# *Life During the* Highland

Cover picture: Sheep grazing in front of the ruins of a crofting township in Wester Ross.
Inside cover picture: Kylerhea – looking across Sound of Sleat to the mainland.
Title page picture: Loch Bracadale, Isle of Skye.
Text based on *The Highland Clearances* by Donald Gunn and Mari Spankie, published by Wayland in 1993.

First published in 1995 by Wayland (Publishers) Ltd,
61 Western Road, Hove, East Sussex BN3 1JD, England.
© Copyright 1995 Wayland (Publishers) Ltd

British Library Cataloguing in Publication Data
Gunn, Donald
    *Life During the Highland Clearances.-*
    Rev.ed
    I. Title II.Spankie, Mari III. Stephen, Margaret
    333.314115

ISBN 0 7502 1532 1

Consultant: Donald Gunn, BBC Education Officer
Editors: Joanna Bentley and Marcella Forster
Designer: Joyce Chester
Printed and bound by B.P.C. Paulton Books, Great Britain

To the reader:
This is an information book. You may wish to read it from beginning to end, but you may choose only to read certain pages to answer your questions or to find the information you require. Don't forget to look at the pictures. They tell you about the Clearances too.

To the teacher:
Most benefit will be derived from this text if pupils are introduced to the topic and its specialized vocabulary before reading takes place. Where background knowledge has been gleaned from related materials, such as television programmes or computer packages, young people will be in a better position not only to use books to find information they require but also to pose their own questions.

Group discussion sessions provide a worthwhile introduction to the information book. Initial examination of layout, illustration and text in the group situation will provide individuals with the confidence to access information.
This text can be used alongside the original to ensure that all pupils have the opportunity to read and learn.

# Clearances

## Contents

# The Ross-shire Sheep Riot

In the year 1792, four hundred men gathered at the River Oykel, in Ross-shire, in the Scottish Highlands. They were there to drive as many sheep as they could find away from the lands that they farmed.

These sheep were called Cheviots. They belonged to the landowners, who had brought in this new breed of large sheep so that they could make a lot of money from sheep farming.

The Gaels, the people who lived in the Highlands, knew that if the sheep stayed on the land the people would have to leave. So, they joined together to try to drive the sheep off the land.

The government, in London, sent soldiers from the Black Watch regiment to stop the riots. But, by the time the soldiers arrived from Edinburgh, the Gaels had gone and the sheep were asleep.

An officer of the 42nd Black Watch regiment reported on the sheep riot. He said that there had been no fighting and the sheep had not suffered at all. Although the rioters had been hungry, they had not taken any sheep for food.

No real harm had been done, but the riot leaders were rounded up and taken to Inverness to be tried. Their punishment was to be put in prison or to be sent overseas. But the men escaped. A reward was offered for their capture but they were never caught.

After that, people were afraid to riot again. They went back to their glens and waited until the landowners turned them out of their homes.

To find out more about the Highland Clearances we need to look back at earlier Scottish history.

▲ An officer of the Black Watch in 1792.

# Who are the Gaels?

Gaelic is a Celtic language. As you will see on the map below, Celtic people lived in many parts of Europe. The Gaels are the people who moved to Scotland from Ireland about 1,500 years ago, bringing their Gaelic language with them. We can tell where they settled by looking closely at place names to find their Gaelic roots.

| Gaelic word | English meaning | Seen on English maps as | Example of place name |
|---|---|---|---|
| achadh | field | auch/ach/auquh | **Auch**inleck |
| baile | farming village | bal | **Bal**erno |
| ceann | head | kin/ken | **Kin**ross |
| cill | church | kil/keil | **Kil**marnock |
| druim | hill ridge | drum | Oldmel**drum** |
| dùn | fort | dun/dum/doon | **Dun**bar |
| inbhir | river-mouth | inner/inver | **Inner**leithen |
| tulach | knoll | tilli/tully | **Tilli**coultry |

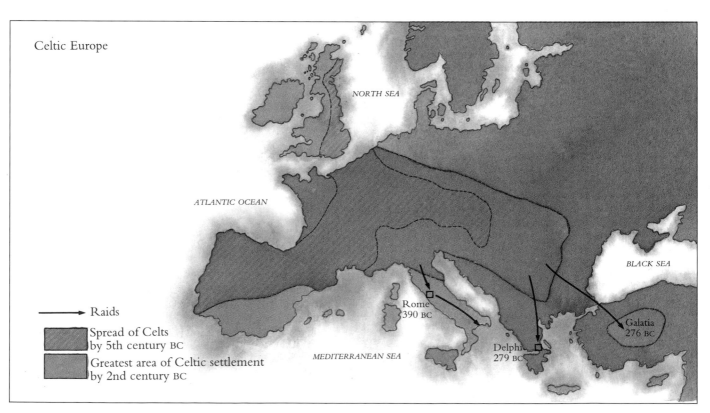

Celtic Europe

NORTH SEA

ATLANTIC OCEAN

BLACK SEA

Rome 390 BC

Galatia 276 BC

Delphi 279 BC

MEDITERRANEAN SEA

→ Raids

Spread of Celts by 5th century BC

Greatest area of Celtic settlement by 2nd century BC

Later, Lowland Scots began to speak more like the English. They thought that Highland people – the Gaels – were rough barbarians.

The Highlanders, in their galleys (ships), did fight the Vikings but Gaels were also proud of their poetry, their music, their art and their crafts. In the Highlands there were libraries full of valuable books.

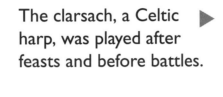

The clarsach, a Celtic harp, was played after feasts and before battles. ▶

In the twelfth century the Gaels sailed in galleys like this one to defeat the Vikings in their longboats. ▼

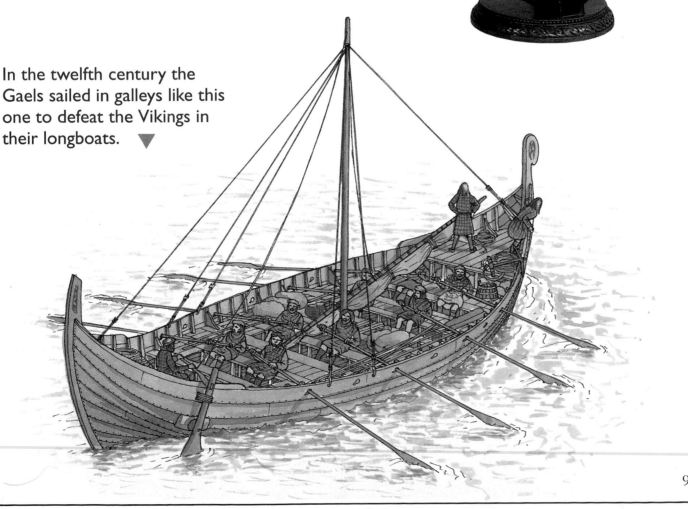

9

# A Divided Nation

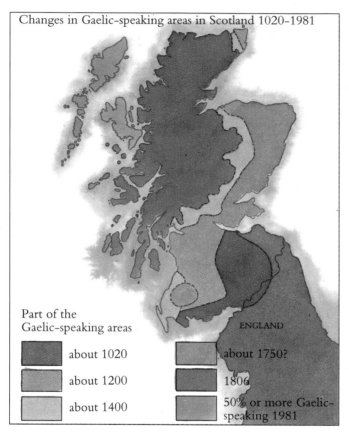

Changes in Gaelic-speaking areas in Scotland 1020-1981

ENGLAND

Part of the Gaelic-speaking areas

| | |
|---|---|
| about 1020 | about 1750? |
| about 1200 | 1806 |
| about 1400 | 50% or more Gaelic-speaking 1981 |

▲ At one time almost all the people in Scotland spoke Gaelic. Now Gaelic is spoken mainly in the area shaded purple.

**The decline of the Gaelic language**.

Two hundred and fifty years ago, one third of the population of Scotland lived in the Highlands. The islands and glens were bustling, lively places. If you had lived in the Highlands then, you would have spoken Gaelic yourself.

Over the years, as more and more Lowlanders spoke English, they grew apart from the Gaelic-speaking Highlanders. There was even a fear in the Lowlands that the Highland chiefs and their armies might march south to attack.

King James VI of Scotland did not understand his Highlanders. He said that there were two kinds of Highlander. The ones who lived on the mainland were quite barbaric, but the ones who lived on the islands in the Hebrides were very barbaric!

▲ James VI of Scotland.

◄ Highland chiefs led thousands of fierce warriors like these.

James VI passed laws to control the Gaels. The sons of Highland chiefs were forced to go south to Lowland schools to learn English. In this way the Gaelic language was used less and less by the leaders, even in the Highlands.

Little by little, Gaelic traditions and culture were pushed out as books, songs and legal papers were written in English.

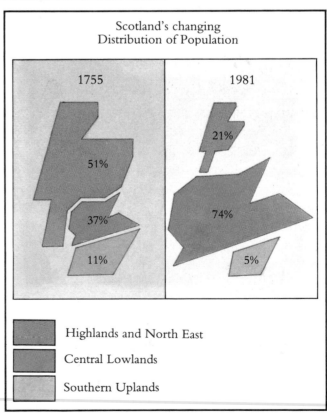

Scotland's changing
Distribution of Population

1755        1981

51%        21%

37%        74%

11%        5%

☐ Highlands and North East

☐ Central Lowlands

☐ Southern Uplands

Before the Clearances, most Scots ▶ lived in the Highlands and North East.

# What was a Clan?

The Gaelic word 'clann' means 'children'. A Scottish clan was like a very large family. Many people had the same surname and lived near each other.

The clan chief was in charge of the 'family'. He looked after his people and they obeyed him. They also fought in his army.

Life was hard for the Highlanders.

◆ As farmers they grew crops and kept cattle.

◆ As traders they drove cattle hundreds of miles to markets in the south. Clansmen also stole cattle from other clans.

◆ As warriors the clansmen fought for their chief in battle. The fighting season was usually the summer.

Women, too, worked on the land, as well as looking after the house and the children.

The Highlanders loved their land. It was a land of songs, stories and clan history.

The chief did not farm the land himself. He divided up the land among close relatives who, in turn, rented small pieces of land to others in the clan.

**The clan system**

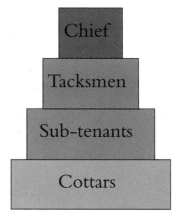

Chief
Tacksmen
Sub-tenants
Cottars

**The Highlanders drove their cattle ▶ south to Lowland markets.**

▲ Chiefs lived in castles. This castle in Moidart is surrounded by water at high tide.

▲ A clan chief in Highland dress.

'Brosnachadh' is a kind of poetry to encourage men before they went into battle.

Here is part of a poem for Clan Donald men before the Battle of Harlaw in 1411. It has been translated from the Gaelic.

*Be vigorous, nimble footed,*
*In winning the battle*
*Against your enemies*
*O Children of Conn of the Hundred Battles.*

# Life in the Glens

Shielings: small stone houses. In summer, cattle were taken to the high pastures. Many township people moved with them for the season.

# The Union with England

In 1603 Queen Elizabeth of England died. She had no children. Because her nearest relative was James VI of Scotland he then also became King James I of England. This was called the Union of the Crowns.

From then on King James VI and I ruled from London. This meant that he was far away from Scotland and especially far away from the Highlands.

Many Scots did not want stronger links with England, but ordinary people had no say in the matter. Important Scots were paid bribes to vote for the Union.

| Bribes paid to important Scottish people. | |
| --- | --- |
| Lord Elibank | £50 |
| Earl of Findlater | £100 |
| Lord Banff | £11 2s |
| Marquis of Montrose | £300 |
| Lord Justice Clerk, Cockburn of Ormiston | £200 |
| Earl of Balcarres | £500 |
| Provost of Wigtown | £25 |
| Lord High Commissioner | £12,325 10s |

Source: Letters published in Memoirs of George Lockhart of Carnwath: Memoirs, 1817.

These were ideas for joining the Scottish and English flags. ▶

Robert Burns (1759–1796), the famous Scottish poet, like many other Scots, did not support the Treaty of Union. In his poem 'A Parcel of Rogues' he says that the people who took bribes to vote for the Union were cowards and traitors.

He shows his anger, but also his pride in Scotland, in these lines:

*Fareweel to a' our Scottish fame,*
*Fareweel our ancient glory!*
*Fareweel ev'n to the Scottish name,*
*Sae famed in martial story!*

▲ Andrew Fletcher was known as 'The Patriot', because he was loyal to Scotland. He spoke out strongly against the Union.

In 1707 Scotland and England were brought closer together when the Treaty of Union was signed. Scotland and England formed a new country called Great Britain. Now they had one British parliament.

Great Britain became a powerful country, but Scots like Andrew Fletcher warned that in a British parliament most of the members would be English. They would not be interested in Scotland.

# The Jacobite Rebellions

The Scottish royal family name was Stuart. King James VII of Scotland and II of England was the grandson of James VI and I. Therefore he was a Stuart.

He was also a Roman Catholic and because of his religion he was forced to give up his throne. His Protestant daughter Mary and her husband, William of Orange, took over the crown.

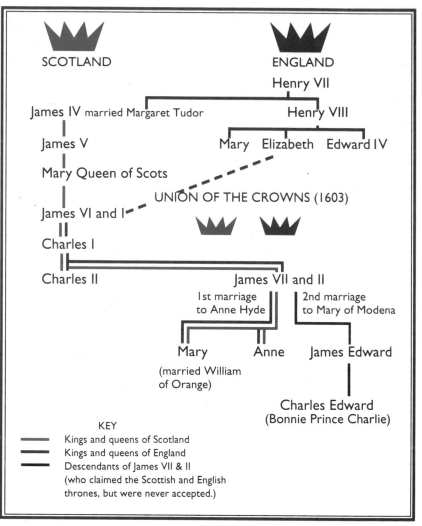

▲ A family tree, showing how the Stuarts came to the English throne.

▲ General Wade is famous for forts, roads and bridges built across the Highlands. They were built to control the Jacobite clans but the roads helped everyone to travel and trade.

The supporters of James were called Jacobites. This word came from Jacobus, the Latin word for James.

The Jacobites tried several times to put the Stuart family back on the throne. The last of these rebellions was in 1745. Some chiefs and clansmen fought and died as Jacobites.

◄ This painting shows a scene at the Battle of Culloden. The 'Forty-five' Rebellion was led by Charles Edward Stuart. He is also known as Bonnie Prince Charlie.

The 1745 rebellion ended in disaster for the Jacobites. They were finally defeated at the Battle of Culloden in 1746.

Gaels in the Highlands suffered. In London they were still seen as barbaric and dangerous. Many Jacobites were killed, put in prison or sent overseas. Highlanders were not allowed to own weapons or to play their bagpipes. They were not allowed to wear the kilt.

Clan tartans, which were so important to the clansmen, were banned. Clan chiefs had their power taken away from them.

The government was getting rid of the clan system.

## The 'Forty-five'
- More Scots fought against Bonnie Prince Charlie than for him.
- At the Battle of Culloden, a third of the government army were Scots, and many Highlanders fought against the Jacobites.

# Highland Life Changes

After 1745 the landlords no longer needed their clansmen to fight.

Things began to change in Scotland. Landlords brought in new ways of farming which produced more food.

◆ The new breeds of sheep were stronger.

◆ Food crops grew well because the land was being drained.

◆ The same crop was no longer grown year after year on the same land. Crops were rotated.

◆ New machines made farm work easier.

There was a great demand for food to feed the large number of people in the Lowlands. Food was also needed for the British armies fighting overseas.

The Highland landlords saw that they could make money for themselves.

**Sheep have taken over areas where people once lived.** ▼

▲The shape of rigs (the old fields, divided into strips) can still be seen on the Isle of Skye.

The ruins of a township that was ▶ cleared in Strathnaver. At one time 100 people lived here.

In some places landlords cleared their clansmen from the land so that they could make larger and better farms. These landlords employed factors, or managers, to run the farms.

Sheep walks were made by joining small townships into very large farms.

The townships were destroyed and the people scattered.

# The Clans are Scattered

Many families lost their homes after sheep were brought to the Highland estates. Large flocks of Cheviots, a new breed of sheep, were put into the sheltered valleys to graze. The people had to leave.

Elizabeth Gordon, Countess of Sutherland, owned a huge estate in the Highlands. She and her husband were very rich people. They owned more than half of the land in Sutherland as well as land in England.

▲ The first Duke of Sutherland.

◀ Dunrobin Castle was the home of the Countess and Duke of Sutherland.

▶ The home of a poor Highlander on the Isle of Skye in 1853.

Letters of that time tell us that the countess and her husband were keen to make changes on their Scottish estates.

The Duke of Sutherland was known as a 'Great Improver', but life was not better for most of the Gaels.

They wanted to:

◆ take away the little patches of land the people farmed;

◆ turn little farms into big sheep farms;

◆ move the Highlanders off their land and send them away to live by the sea.

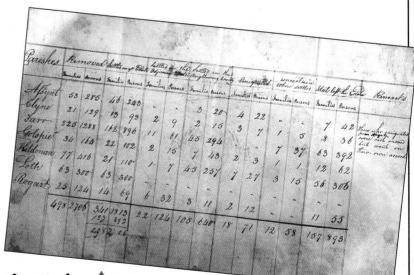

This record from 1819 shows some of the figures for ▲ people who had to move from the Sutherland estate.

# The Sutherland Clearances

James Loch was the factor who ran the estates of the Duke and Countess of Sutherland. He cleared many people from the glens in Sutherland.

Over 14 years, almost half the people in Sutherland were evicted. Loch carried out his duties so well that he was hated by most Gaels.

Patrick Sellar was a lawyer who worked for the Countess of Sutherland, collecting rents and checking up on tenants. He did not like the Gaels any more than James Loch did.

In 1814, which was remembered as the Year of the Burnings, Sellar had all the tenants in Strathnaver thrown out.

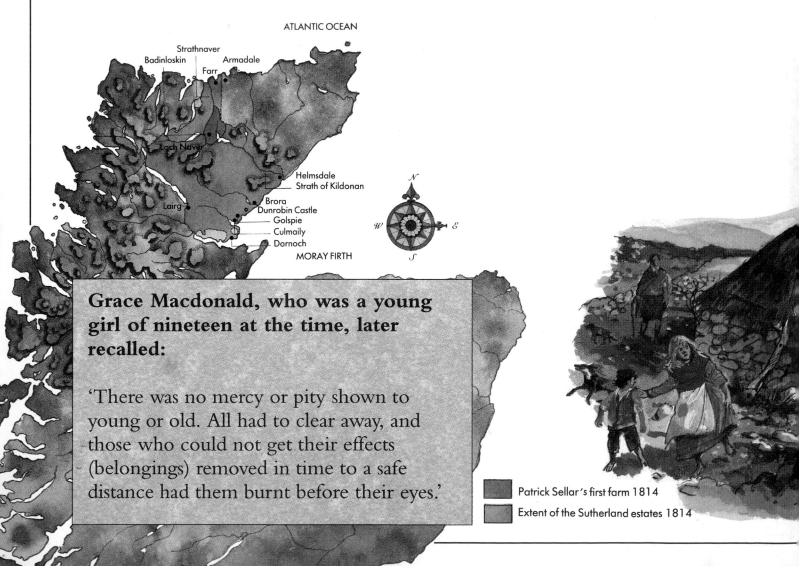

**Grace Macdonald, who was a young girl of nineteen at the time, later recalled:**

'There was no mercy or pity shown to young or old. All had to clear away, and those who could not get their effects (belongings) removed in time to a safe distance had them burnt before their eyes.'

Patrick Sellar's first farm 1814

Extent of the Sutherland estates 1814

The grazing areas were burned so that there was no grass for the cattle to eat. Houses were burned so that people had to leave.

Donald MacLeod, a Gael, wrote:

'I was present at the pulling down and burning of the house of William Chisholm, (of) Badinloskin, in which was lying his wife's mother, an old bedridden woman of near 100 years of age. . . I told him (Sellar) of the poor old woman. . . He replied, "Damn her, the old witch; she has lived too long. Let her burn!". . . She died within five days.'

(From *Gloomy Memories*, Donald MacLeod, 1857.)

▼ Patrick Sellar, later in life.

### Patrick Sellar

In 1816 Sellar was tried for murder and fire-raising. The jury found him not guilty. James Loch wrote to the Countess of Sutherland telling her that Sellar had treated people harshly, but Sellar still went on to become a rich landowner.

◀ Patrick Sellar watches the burning of William Chisholm's house.

25

# Why was there no Revolution?

▲ In Strathcarron in Ross-shire, in 1854, police beat and kicked
women who tried to stay in their homes.

The Gaels were treated very badly. It, therefore, seems surprising that they did not join together to rebel. There were many reasons why this did not happen.

◆ The Gaels had nothing to fight with. Their weapons had been taken away after the 'Forty-five' rebellion.

◆ They knew that the government soldiers could be very cruel. Sometimes soldiers were sent to evict people. Sometimes police were sent.

◆ The Gaels had no leaders. They still obeyed their clan chiefs but their chiefs no longer supported them.

The church did not help the Gaels. The Highlanders were religious people. They went to their church ministers for help but they were told not to fight. The ministers wanted to please the landowners so they did not speak out against the evictions.

In 1845 people who used to attend Croick Church went back to camp in the churchyard after they were evicted. The sad messages they scratched on the windows can still be seen today.

A reporter from the *Times* newspaper described the scene:

'A fire was kindled in the churchyard round which the poor children

▲ Croick Church, Strathcarron, Ross-shire.

clustered. Two cradles with infants in them were placed close to the fire, and sheltered round by the dejected-looking mothers.'

◀ A family being evicted from their home.

# Emigration and Famine

◀ The title of this painting is *The Last of the Clan*. The Highlanders are sad to say goodbye to family and friends who are emigrating.

Clearances took place right across the Highlands and Islands. Many people emigrated, leaving by ship to go to the 'New World'. They were looking for a better life, but first they had to endure a desperate journey.

◆ Ship owners overcrowded their ships to make more money.

◆ The ships did not leave on time. Sometimes they were days late. When passengers' food ran out, they had to buy more at high prices.

◆ Once on the ship poor people lived in filthy conditions. Because of this people got terrible diseases, such as smallpox.

Many people died before the ships arrived in the New World.

Thousands of people left the Highlands, but still the population grew. Families were very large at that time. In some places people were crowded together on the coast with very little land for growing crops.

The potato had become the main food of the Highlanders. In 1846 most potato crops were destroyed by a disease called 'potato blight'. The people went hungry. They had to be given help, otherwise they would have starved.

Highlanders emigrated to countries like Canada and Australia. Their fares were paid by the government, by charities and sometimes by landlords. It was cheaper to pay fares than to take care of poor people in the Highlands.

Inverness Courier  28 May 1845

EMIGRATION

At Glasgow for New York
By American Passenger Packet Ship
Warsaw
600 tons burthen
N.T. Hawkins, Commander
who is well known in the trade for his care and attention to passengers, will be ready to receive goods in a few days, and be despatched positively on 15 June.
This fine vessel has great height between Decks, and in every respect suitable and superior accommodation for cabin, Intermediate and Steerage Passengers, as she will be fitted up on the most approved principle, according to Act of Parliament, and Emigrants may rely on every attention being paid to their health and comfort. Immediate application is recommended.
For freight or passage, apply to:
C.J. Bancks, 130 Broomielaw.
N.B. The usual allowances of Bread and Potatoes; Tea, Sugar, Tobacco &c free of Duty.
Glasgow 22 May 1845

▲ An emigration advert. Shipping agents tried to reassure emigrants that conditions on board would be good.

◄ The *Hercules* in the harbour at Campbeltown with emigrants from the Isle of Skye, in January 1853.

# Where did the People Go?

People who left the Highlands did one of four things:

◆ they went to the coast to live by the sea;

◆ they went to live in cities in the Lowlands;

◆ they joined the army;

◆ they went abroad to live in another country.

## THE COAST

Some people who were thrown off their land went to live near the sea. There they lived on small farms called crofts. These new crofts were often on rocky ground on the top of high cliffs. The soil was too poor for people to grow enough food crops to feed their families and pay rent.

**INVERNESS COURIER**
September 1829

**HERRING FISHING – SIX MEN DROWNED**

On the evening of Monday 24 August, the fishing boats at Wick went out as usual in quest of herring. During the night a very strong breeze sprang up from the north-west, which scattered most of the boats up and down the firth; and lamentable to relate, one of the boats, belonging to Pulteney, has not been heard of since.

▲This newspaper report tells of a fishing boat accident.

◄ When families lived here little children could not play freely in case they fell over the edge of the cliff.

Kelpers on the Isle of Skye. Many people worked up to their waists in water, cutting the seaweed. ▶

It was difficult for people who had always been farmers to find other work at the coast.

At first, there was work for a large number of people on the west coast and islands. Many people were needed to gather seaweed, which was called kelp. It was used to make soap, glass and fertilizer. For a time, the landlords who owned the kelp made a lot of money, but they paid the kelpers very little. Because people had no other way of making a living, they had to gather kelp.

Suddenly the kelp industry failed. No one wanted Scottish kelp.

More money could be made from sheep. Again, crofters were forced to leave their homes. Only a few stayed.

Crofts at the coast. ▶

# THE LOWLANDS

Many families moved to the cities. They went to cities like Glasgow. There they looked for work in cotton mills, on the railways, in coal mines and ship-building yards. The cities grew so quickly that housing conditions were very bad.

The box below shows the growing number of people living in Glasgow between 1780 and 1871.

| Growth of Glasgow | | | |
|---|---|---|---|
| 1780 | 1811 | 1841 | 1871 |
| 42,000 | 100,700 | 274,000 | 477,700 |

The newcomers lived in the poorest parts of the city. There was no proper water supply. There were no drains or sewers like we have today. Rubbish was just left to pile up in the streets. Rents were not cheap, and families often had to share rooms.

▲ Slum tenement housing in Glasgow in 1868.

◄ A shipyard on the River Clyde in 1878. Highlanders found work helping to build ships.

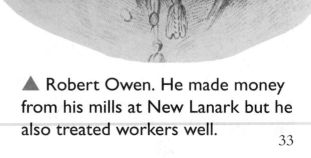

▲ New Lanark was founded by David Dale in 1785. Workers here had good working and living conditions.

Diseases such as cholera, typhus and smallpox killed many people. They spread quickly because people lived in crowded and dirty conditions.

The newcomers made friends at Gaelic clubs and chapels set up by Highlanders already in the cities. A large number of people in Glasgow spoke Gaelic as their first language before English.

But some people found a good life in the Lowlands. At New Lanark, David Dale and Robert Owen owned the cotton mills. They looked after their workers. Every Highlander who worked for them was given a house at a low rent and good working conditions.

▲ Robert Owen. He made money from his mills at New Lanark but he also treated workers well.

# THE ARMED FORCES

Many thousands of men left the Scottish Highlands to fight for Britain. Clan chiefs were given money by the government in London to form regiments of Highland soldiers.

Men joined the army for a number of reasons.

◆ Some men joined because they were loyal to the clan.

◆ Many joined because they were afraid that, if they did not, the chief would force their parents out of their homes.

◆ Others were proud to wear the kilt and it was only in the British army that they were allowed to wear it in the years between 1746 and 1782.

Major General James Wolfe saw the Highlanders fight at the Battle of Culloden. He wanted Highlanders to help fight the French in North America because they were used to rough country and were strong and fearless. But secretly he did not care how many died in battle and very many did die.

Major General Wolfe, leading a successful attack on Quebec, Canada, in 1759. Many Highlanders were in the army. Here, half of the British soldiers killed were Highlanders. ▼

▲ This brave soldier is wounded but still plays his pipes to encourage his comrades.

## Highland regiments

● By about 1830, one third of the British Army came from the Highlands.

● After the Clearances, Highlanders were not keen to join the army. In Sutherland the men said:

'We have no country to fight for. You robbed us of our country and gave it to the sheep. Therefore, since you have preferred sheep to men, let sheep defend you.'

(From *The Northern Ensign*, Donald Ross.)

Usually Highland soldiers had the best discipline in the British army. They looked after each other and did not forget their families at home. Even an enemy of Britain, like Emperor Napoleon of France, admired their bravery.

However, there were times when the government broke promises to the Highland regiments. Then the Highlanders rose up and mutinied.

# ABROAD

Thousands of Highland families went abroad to other countries to find a better life. In Scotland they left behind deserted lands.

They went all over the world but especially to the 'new' countries you can see on the map below. There was plenty of land there for the Highlanders and other emigrants. There are towns, rivers and mountains in those countries with Scottish names given to them by settlers to remind them of home.

Letters from the New World told of an exciting life. More Highlanders emigrated to join friends and relatives.

◀ This piper is in Virginia, USA. Highland culture has spread all over the world.

◀ This map of the world shows where most of the emigrants from Scotland went.

The gravestone of an emigrant, at Prince Edward Island in Canada. ▼

▲ This drawing shows emigrants who went to Canada in 1878 to start a new life. They built their own homes and set up farms where no one had farmed before.

Sometimes large groups from the same town sailed together to build a new life abroad.

But life there could be hard too. People had to clear land for their own farms. It was not easy to find food. There were not enough tools for building and farming. The people who already lived there were not always friendly.

The Highlanders who emigrated took their traditions with them. Religion and education were still very important to them. The Highland emigrants added a great deal to the life of their new countries.

## Important Gaels

**Alexander Mackenzie** was born on the Isle of Lewis. He emigrated to Canada, where he explored large areas of the country. The Mackenzie River was named after him.

**John A. Macdonald** travelled to Canada as a boy. He worked to bring parts of Canada together and became the first prime minister of the whole of Canada.

# The Crofters' War

▲ Carl Haag's water-colour painting *Morning in the Highlands* shows Queen Victoria and her royal party. She made the Highlands a fashionable place for the wealthy to visit.

Queen Victoria built a castle at Balmoral in 1855. The Highlands then became very popular with tourists, who came by train and by steamboat. But it was only rich people who came on holiday.

They came to large estates where they could shoot deer on the hills and catch fish in the rivers. The landowners now made more money from the estates than from sheep. Wool from abroad was cheaper than Scots wool.

◀ Protesting crofters confront the law on the Isle of Lewis. (From the *Illustrated London News*, 1888.)

Again, the people who suffered terribly were the crofters.

By 1880 the crofters had lost so much land that they rose up against the landowners. They joined groups called Land Leagues to try to change the law. They wanted to save the Highland traditions and Gaelic culture.
By this time the crofters had strong leaders and good support.

◆ Gaels who had gone to the cities helped them.

◆ Church ministers spoke up for them.

◆ They even had Members of Parliament elected from their group.

Men and women fought with police. They were no longer going to keep quiet as their parents had done. They fought for their rights.

At last, in 1886, the government passed the Crofter Act. As a result, crofters could no longer be evicted or asked to pay unfair rents. But the land was not returned to the people.

Even many years later, crofters were still trying to get back some of their land.

A crofters' leader speaks at a meeting on the Isle of Skye. (From the *Illustrated London News*, 1884.) ▶

# The Highlands Today

▲ Animals such as these deer are protected on the Isle of Rum. Rum is now a Nature Reserve. Once crofters grew their crops here.

Landowners still own large, empty areas of land in the Highlands.

Over the years the environment has been damaged in many ways.

◆ Sheep choose the best grass to eat. This means that rough plants take over.

◆ When there are too many deer they destroy young trees.

◆ The land has also been damaged when people set fire to the moorland in spring. They burn the land to help fresh new plants to grow. But sometimes the fires get out of control. The plants are then destroyed.

As a result of all this damage many parts of the Highlands today are bare and bleak.

Today there are new ideas for using the land.

◆ Large numbers of people like to ski and to climb in the Highlands.

◆ There are people who want to bring more tourists to the hotels.

◆ New factories and craft workshops could give work to local people.

◆ Many groups think that the government should buy land so that it can be properly cared for.

There are still some crofting communities but they are small. Growing crops and keeping cattle do not spoil the environment, but there is not enough work to keep the young people on the crofts. They have had to leave the Highlands to find jobs.

In Assyn in Sutherland, some crofters joined together to buy an estate but they needed help from supporters. Most crofters do not have the money to compete with the rich outsiders who buy land in the Highlands.

▲ Burning the land on moors and hills (called muirburn).

◀ Crofting today on the Isle of Skye.

# Glossary

**Cottars** The farm hands and families who worked the land for the tenant farmers.

**Crofts** Small farms of a few acres of land. People who work crofts are called crofters.

**Crop rotation** A system of farming in which the crop that is grown in a field is changed from year to year, to keep the soil healthy.

**Emigration** Leaving your home country.

**Eviction** The forcible moving of people, by law, out of houses and off the land.

**Factor** The word used in Scotland for an estate manager.

**Gaelic** The language of the Gaels. It is still spoken in Scotland and abroad.

**Gaels** One of the Celtic family of peoples. They settled in Scotland, Ireland, and the Isle of Man, and were the original Scots.

**Jacobites** Supporters of the Stuarts, the Scottish royal family

**Mutiny** An uprising against authority, usually in the armed forces.

**New World** The old term for North and South America.

**Rebellion** An uprising against the government.

**Sheep walks** Large sheep farms, made by joining the old, small townships together

**Tacksmen** The men who leased out land for their chiefs to the tenant farmers. They collected rents and shared out the land.

**Tenant** A person who pays rent for land or property.

Picture acknowledgements
The publishers would like to thank the following for providing the illustrations: City of Edinburgh Museums & Art Galleries/Bridgeman Art Library, London 11 (Sir Joseph Paton's *At Bay*), 12 (*All Hallows Fair* by Howe, James 1780-1836); City of York Art Gallery/Bridgeman Art Library 20 (Richard Andsell's *Drovers in Glen Sligichan, Isle of Skye*); Peter Duncan 40, 41 (top); David Gowans 41 (bottom); By courtesy of Edinburgh City Libraries 31 (top); Mary Evans Picture Library 10, 22 (top), 23 (top), 32 (bottom), 37 (left), 38 (bottom), 39; Glasgow Museums: Art Gallery & Museum, Kelvingrove 28 (Thomas Faed's *The Last of the Clan*); Donald Gunn 21 (bottom), 27 (top); Hulton Deutsch Collection 29; Cailean Maclean cover, endpaper, title page, 21 (top), 31 (bottom), 37 (right) 41 (bottom); Mansell 17, 32 (top), 33 (both), 34; Scottish National Portrait Gallery 13 (bottom), (*Sir Murray Mungo*, by John Michael Wright), 18 (*Field Marshall George Wade*, attrib. J van Diest); Trustees of the National Library of Scotland 16, 25; Trustees of the National Library of Scotland and the Sutherland Estates Office 23 (bottom); Trustees of the National Museums of Scotland 7, 9, 27 (bottom); Photri 36 (top, J McCauley); The Royal Collection © 1993 Her Majesty the Queen 19 (David Morier's *A Jacobite Incident: Culloden*), 38 (top, Carl Haag's *Morning in the Highlands*); Jo Scott/Dunbeath Preservation Trust 30; STB/Still Moving Pic Co 13 (top, Paul Tomkins), 22 (bottom, Doug Corrance).
Artwork was supplied by: Sallie Alane Reason 8, 10, 11, 24, 36, 44; Gavin Rowe 6, 25, 26; Mike Taylor cover, 9, 14-15. Thanks to Charles W J Withers 1984 *Gaelic in Scotland 1698-1981: The geographical history of a Language* (Edinburgh, John Donald), for the map reference on page 10. Thanks also to Rob Gibson for the use of his diagram for page 11. The diorama showing Life in the Glens on pages 14-15 is based on artwork by Richard Proudfoot now owned by 'Landmarks'.

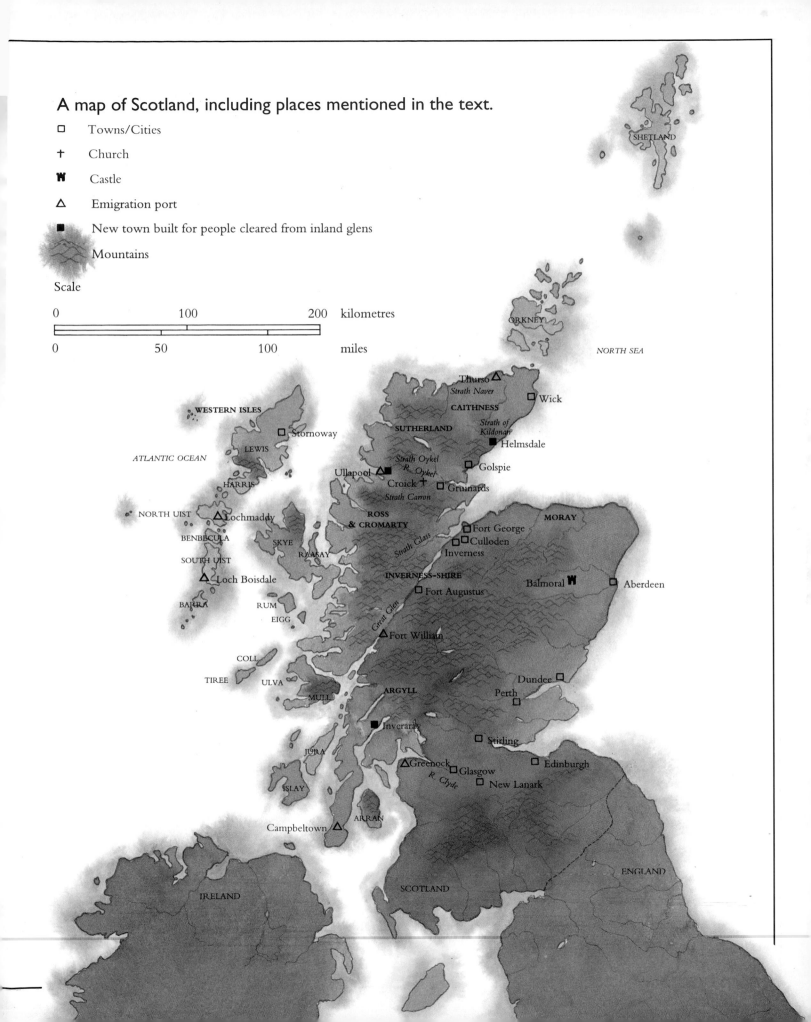

# A map of Scotland, including places mentioned in the text.

- □ Towns/Cities
- † Church
- ♖ Castle
- △ Emigration port
- ■ New town built for people cleared from inland glens
- Mountains

Scale

0       100       200    kilometres

0       50       100    miles

SHETLAND

ORKNEY

NORTH SEA

Thurso △
*Strath Naver*
Wick
CAITHNESS
*Strath of Kildonan*
SUTHERLAND
Helmsdale
WESTERN ISLES
Stornoway
*Strath Oykel*
*R. Oykel*
Golspie
LEWIS
Ullapool △
ATLANTIC OCEAN
Croick †
Gruinards
*Strath Carron*
HARRIS
ROSS & CROMARTY
MORAY
NORTH UIST
△ Lochmaddy
Fort George
Culloden
BENBECULA
SKYE
Inverness
*Strath Glass*
SOUTH UIST
RAASAY
△ Loch Boisdale
INVERNESS-SHIRE
Balmoral ♖
Aberdeen
BARRA
RUM
*Great Glen*
△ Fort William
EIGG
COLL
TIREE
ULVA
Dundee
MULL
ARGYLL
Perth
■ Inveraray
Stirling
JURA
△ Greenock
Glasgow
Edinburgh
*R. Clyde*
New Lanark
ISLAY
ARRAN
Campbeltown △
IRELAND
SCOTLAND
ENGLAND

# Further Information

**Books to read**
**Non fiction:**
Highland Clearances Trail – a guide, Rob Gibson (Highland Heritage, Tir nan Oran, 8 Culcairn Road, Evanton, Ross-shire IV16 9YT). ISBN 0950 9882 35
This is a guidebook to clearance sites throughout Scotland. It contains clear map references and a bibliography suitable for adults.

**Fiction:**
*The Desperate Journey*, Kathleen Fidler (Canongate Press, 1987)
*Ribbon of Fire,* Allan Campbell McLean (Canongate Press, 1985)
*So Far From Skye,* Judith O'Neill (Puffin Books, 1993)
*A Sound of Trumpets*, Allan Campbell McLean (Canongate Press, 1985)
*The Story of Ranald*, Griselda Gifford (Canongate Press, 1985)
*A Pistol in Greenyards*, Mollie Hunter (Canongate Press, 1988)

Most non-fiction books on the Clearances have been written for adults. However, museums and visitor centres often offer appropriate pupil material or experiences. For further information contact:
Highland Folk Museum (Regional Museum of Countrylife), Duke Street, Kingussie PH21 1JG.
National Museum of Antiquities, 1 Queen Street, Edinburgh.
Caithness and Sutherland Tourist Board, The Square, Dornoch, Sutherland IV25 3SD.
Auchindrain, Inverary, Argyll PA32 8XN. (Auchindrain is a West Highland farming township that survived until the 1960s.)

Jordanhill Campus, University of Strathclyde, has a computer-assisted topic called *Desperate Journey*, available through their educational catalogue from:
Sales & Publications, Jordanhill Campus, 76 Southbrae Drive, Glasgow G13 1PP.

BBC Education Scotland have produced the following two units of programmes on the Clearances (transmissions Autumn 1993). For TV – *Clearances,* in *Around Scotland* (also made in Gaelic). For radio – *The Desperate Journey,* in *Scottish Resources* 10-12.
Print support and BBC software is available from: BBC Education Scotland, 5 Queen Street, Edinburgh EH2 1JF.

# Index

Numbers in bold refer to illustrations as well as text.